A Simple Guide to Life

Robert Bogoda

Buddhist Publication Society
Kandy • Sri Lanka

Published in 1994

Buddhist Publication Society
P.O. Box 61
54, Sangharaja Mawatha
Kandy, Sri Lanka

Copyright © 1994 by Robert Bogoda

ISBN 955-24-0125-9

Typeset at the BPS
Text set in Galliard

Printed in Sri Lanka by
Karunaratne & Sons Ltd.
647, Kularatne Mawatha
Colombo 10

THE WHEEL PUBLICATION NO. 397/398

Contents

Introduction 1
1. The Right View of Life 5
2. Benefits of Right Understanding 12
3. A Life Plan 16
4. Obstacles 18
5. Relaxation 20
6. Observing the Five Precepts 22
7. Controlling the Emotions 25
8. Beware of Bias and Propaganda 28
9. A Happy Family Life 30
10. The Practice of Benevolence 36
11. Freeing the Mind 38
12. Mindfulness of Breathing 42
13. Facing Death with Equanimity 43
14. The Good Buddhist 45
    About the Author 48

Introduction

Innumerable books have been written about Buddhism, but most of these are far too exhaustive, too specialized, or too scholarly to be of much practical help to the busy lay Buddhist in search of concise guidance. A short, clear, and simple handbook on how to live a proper Buddhist lay life was therefore a much felt need. The present essay attempts to fill that gap by providing exactly what its title offers: A Simple Guide to Life.

For easy reference the essay has been divided into short, convenient sections. The first section is theoretical in emphasis. It attempts to fix in the reader's mind the essential principles of the Buddha's teaching, without complicated and sophisticated explanations. The principles discussed here should serve as a clear-cut philosophy of life, a framework which illuminates the meaning and purpose of the Buddhist life. These principles will enable the lay Buddhist to understand his or her place in the larger scheme of things, to order priorities, and to devise a proper way to achieve them. The lack of a clear philosophy of life, so widespread today, is largely responsible for the steady decline in ethical standards, both individually and socially, in Sri Lanka and in the world as a whole.

The second section is concerned with the practical implications of adopting the understanding of existence sketched in the first section. We here examine the visible benefits of accepting the Buddha-Dhamma as a way of thinking and living; in this section we will also throw a sidelong glance at what happens to a society when spiritual values are abandoned in favour of an exclusive stress on material development.

The next two sections discuss respectively the need to draw up an individual life plan and the obstacles likely to impede the successful implementation of that plan. The central problem of a Buddhist lay follower is to combine a successful lay life with Buddhist moral and spiritual principles. This problem can be solved by organizing one's life as a lay Buddhist within the framework of the Noble Eightfold Path, which represents the Master's teaching in practice. Because some degree of economic security is essential to growth in the Dhamma, the Buddha was concerned with the material welfare of his lay disciples as much as with their spiritual development. He did not deter them from seeking mundane happiness, but he stressed that in pursuing mundane goals, the lay Buddhist should take great care to avoid breaking the basic rules of morality. These rules are summed up in the Five Precepts of virtue, the minimum code of ethics to be followed by a Buddhist householder. As the Five Precepts are thus of such fundamental importance to a Buddhist lay follower, a separate section is devoted to discussing them.

The remaining sections of the essay show how to apply the basic principles of Buddhism to the other major areas of a Buddhist householder's life. The essay ends with a section briefly describing what is expected of an ideal lay Buddhist in daily life. The guiding maxim of the entire essay is: A little well done is better than a lot poorly done.

To sum up: The Buddha's teaching, which is unique in its completeness, is the most rational and consistent plan for wholesome living. It is not based on dogma or blind faith, but on facts and verifiable conclusions. It therefore offers a

Introduction

reasonable way of life which should be attractice to any thinking person. Moreover, the Dhamma is completely compatible with the advances of modern science and does not require clever reinterpretations to avoid clashes with scientific discoveries.

The mere fact of accepting Buddhism intellectually, however, will not ensure happiness and security. To yield its fruit the Buddha's teaching has to be utilized intelligently and constructively in all the activities of our daily life. It has to be adopted, adapted, and applied until all its basic principles are absorbed and made habitual by repeated practice, for a theoretical knowledge of Buddhism is insufficient in itself.

If one wishes to make changes in the changing personality that one now is, these changes will take time and patience. The lofty heights of Nibbāna are not to be reached by a sudden leap but by quiet, persistent endeavour over a long period, guided by the Master's teaching. Let us not forget that a journey of a thousand miles begins with a single step. Daily practice, beginning with the strict observance of the Five Precepts, is the way to orderly progress along the path. Even a little practice every day brings the practitioner a little nearer to the goal each day.

I take this opportunity to offer the merit of this gift of Dhamma most gratefully and most devotedly to my parents, now no more. Such a gift excels all other gifts: Sabbadānaṁ dhammadānaṁ jināti. May it redound to their happiness.

A Simple Guide to Life

1. The Right View of Life

To be happy, successful, and secure, we must first learn to see ourselves and the world as they truly are and should then shape our everyday activities in keeping with this view. We must also look for solutions to our problems in terms of the relationship of cause and effect, for the universal law of causality operates in the field of human behaviour as much as it does in the physical world.

The foundation for a fruitful life is an understanding of the moral law of kamma. Kamma is volitional action, action that expresses morally determinate intentions or volitions. We need to recognize clearly that wholesome and unwholesome deeds produce corresponding good and bad results. As a person sows, so shall he reap. Good begets good, and evil begets evil. This retributive power is inherent in volitional action or kamma.

Kamma is also cumulative. Not only do our deeds generate pleasant and painful results, but in their cumulative force they also determine our character. The deeds we perform in any one life are transmitted to future lives in the form of dispositions. These dispositions constitute our character traits.

Inherent in the action is the power of producing its due result. This happens without the intervention or help of any external agency. Buddhism denies the existence of a Creator-God. Kamma is neither fate nor predestination, but our own willed action considered as capable of producing results. Understanding the kammic moral law of cause and effect, we will learn to control our actions in order to serve our own welfare as well as to promote the good of others.

There are ten unwholesome courses of action (akusala-kammapatha), deeds which originate from the defilements of greed, hatred, and delusion. These are: killing, stealing, sexual misconduct, lying, slander, harsh speech, useless talk, covetousness, ill will, and false views. Contrary to these, there are ten bases of merit (*puññakiriya-vatthu*), deeds which spring from the virtuous qualities of detachment, goodwill, and wisdom, and which generate wholesome kamma: generosity, morality, meditation, reverence, service, transference of merit, rejoicing in the good deeds of others, hearing the Dhamma, expounding the Dhamma, and straightening out one's views.

It is lack of right understanding and ignorance of the underlying laws of life that account for the prevalence of materialism in today's world, even in the traditional homelands of the Buddha-Dhamma. When people become convinced that everything perishes at death, they lose sight of lofty ethical ideals and become indifferent to the long-range consequences of their deeds. Their entire lives revolve around the blind pursuit of sensual pleasures. Thus we find that today people worship money regardless of how it is earned, hunt for pleasure no matter where it is found, chase power and fame regardless of the cost to their personal integrity.

Ignorance of the law is no valid excuse in a court of law, and so it is with regard to the moral law of kamma: the law operates regardless of whether one believes in it or not, due effects following from their respective causes. Just as an infant will get burnt if it touches fire regardless of whether or not it understands the dangers in playing with fire, so those who violate the laws of morality will have to face the conse-

The Right View of Life

quences when their kamma ripens, regardless of whether or not they accept the teaching of kamma.

Just as a shadow is connected with an object, so is rebirth connected with kamma. Craving (*taṇhā*), selfish desire, prompts us to do life-affirming deeds, kamma, volitional action. No force in nature is ever lost, and moral energy is no exception. So long as craving and ignorance remain in the mind, kamma must find expression at death. The inevitable fruit of craving for existence is rebirth.

Buddhism affirms the continuity of the individual life-flux at death, but denies the existence of a permanent soul. Mind is a flux of mental processes without any persisting core, yet this flux, though insubstantial, continues from life to life as long as it is driven on by the thirst for more becoming. The mind of a dying person, owing to the latent craving for continued existence, grasps at some object, idea, or feeling connected with an action done during his lifetime, and this grasping vitalizes an appropriate germ of life. The new form of life may be human or non-human, in keeping with the kamma or moral forces generated during the deceased's lifetime. The germ of life kindled by the process of rebirth is endowed with an initial consciousness (called the paṭisandhicitta) in which lie latent all the past impressions, characteristics, and tendencies of that particular individual. Hence death leads to birth and birth to death. Rebirth is thus possible without a transmigrating soul.

The twin Buddhist doctrines of kamma and rebirth are the "middle way" that provides a satisfactory answer to the problem of life. The middle way avoids the extremes of theism and materialism, preserving moral accountability without the problems raised by positing an almighty yet benevolent God. A human being is the visible expression of his or her own past action. One is born from one's past kamma, supported by one's present kamma, and at death goes where one's accumulated kamma leads one.

Buddhism teaches that human beings evolve according to the quality of the kamma they have performed during their lifetime. This supplies a rational basis for morality in place of the commandments of a Creator-God. According to the Buddha's teachings, there can be regression ("kammic descent") from the human plane to subhuman realms such as the animal world, and progress ("kammic ascent") from the human plane to the heavenly planes. Taking into account the dangers of a fall to subhuman realms, one should always act with care. Virtue, based on a righteous code of conduct, protects one from regression and ensures spiritual progress.

A true follower of the Buddha accepts the moral law of kamma as just, recognizing it as the chief reason for the many inequalities among human beings in regard to health, wealth, and wisdom. He also learns to face life's losses, disappointments, failures, and adversities calmly, without complaining; for he knows that they are the result of his own past misdeeds. If he asks himself: "Why has this happened to me?" the answer will be expressed in terms of action and result. He will try to solve his problems to the best of his ability and will adjust himself to the new situation when external change is not possible. He will not act rashly, nor fall into despair, nor try to escape his difficulties by resorting to drink, drugs, or suicide, as so often happens in Sri Lanka. Such conduct only shows emotional immaturity and ignorance of the Buddha's teachings.

For a genuine Buddhist, then, one's everyday activities, by way of thought, word, and deed, are more important than anything else in life. A proper understanding of the Bud-

The Right View of Life

dhist moral law of kamma and rebirth is essential for happy and sensible living and for the welfare of the world. In the Buddha's own words:

> The slayer gets a slayer in his turn;
> The conqueror gets one who conquers him;
> The abuser wins abuse, the annoyer frets.
> Thus by the evolution of the deed,
> A man who spoils is spoiled in his turn."
>
> (Saṁyutta Nikāya, Kosala Saṁyutta,
> trans. by Sir Robert Chalmers)

Although we imagine ourselves to be a self—a real substantial individual—according to the Buddha's teaching we are in reality nothing more than a flame-like process, an ever-changing combination of matter and mind, neither of which is the same for two consecutive moments. All the components of our being are impermanent, unsatisfactory, and devoid of self. Life is not a being, an identity, but a becoming; not a product, but a process. There is in actuality no doer, only a doing; no thinker, only a thinking; no goer, only a going.

The Buddha teaches us how to put an end to the beginningless cycle of rebirths in which we undergo the manifold kinds of suffering. The way to end the cycle is by removing the causes that drive it forward life after life. The principal cause is craving, which assumes many forms. Craving impels a person to engage in action (kamma) designed to satisfy the craving, yet as craving is essentially insatiable the result is rebirth.

Craving is a powerful mental force latent in all unenlightened beings. The cause of craving is ignorance (*avijjā*) of the true nature of life: not knowing that life is an ever-changing process, subject to suffering, and totally devoid of a self or core. All life, wherever it is found, bears this same nature: a process stamped with the three marks of impermanence, unsatisfactoriness, and egolessness (*anicca, dukkha, anattā*).

The Buddha realized for himself the true nature of life and through this realization attained to something beyond life and death: a reality that is permanent, blissful, and deathless. This state cannot be described but has to be realized inwardly as a matter of direct personal experience; it has to be attained for oneself and by oneself. This ultimate reality, where thought expires in experience, is Nibbāna, the goal of the Buddhist path.

The Buddha's teachings may thus be condensed into these four verifiable truths, called the Four Noble Truths: suffering, its cause (i.e. craving), its cessation (i.e. Nibbāna), and the way leading to cessation of suffering (i.e. the Noble Eightfold Path). These are eternal truths, truths that do not change and cannot change with time and place.

The only way for us to avoid unhappiness and dissatisfaction is to eliminate the craving that gives birth to it; for everything eagerly sought for and clung to is impermanent. Nothing lasts forever—no person, no object, no experience. Whatever arises must perish, and to cling to the perishable sooner or later ends in suffering. It is by no means easy to eliminate craving; in fact, it is the most difficult challenge of all. But when we do so, we will reach a state of inward perfection and unshakable calm.

We can reach the end of suffering by cultivating the Noble Eightfold Path in its three stages of morality, concentration, and wisdom—*sīla, samādhi, paññā*. Morality purifies conduct and concentration makes the mind calm. When the mind is calm and concentrated, wisdom arises, clear insight,

The Right View of Life

the knowledge and vision of things as they really are. With the arising of wisdom, craving in all its forms is forever destroyed; the flame of life is then extinguished for want of fuel. The Unconditioned has been won—Nibbāna, which is deathless, blissful, and real.

The Noble Eightfold Path consists of the following eight factors, inter-related and inter-connected, ordered into three groups:

Wisdom group (*paññā*)

1. Right understanding: knowledge of the true nature of life; understanding the Four Noble Truths.
2. Right thought: thought free from sensuality, ill-will, and aggression.

Morality group (*sīla*)

3. Right speech: abstinence from falsehood, slander, harsh speech, and useless words.
4. Right action: abstinence from killing, stealing, and sexual misconduct.
5. Right livelihood: avoiding any means of livelihood that involves harm or exploitation of others.

Concentration group (*samādhi*)

6. Right effort: training the mind to avoid unwholesome mental states and to develop wholesome mental states.
7. Right mindfulness: developing the power of attentiveness and awareness in regard to the "four foundations of mindfulness"—body, feelings, mind, and mental phenomena.
8. Right concentration: cultivation of one-pointedness of mind.

These eight factors summarize the Buddha's teaching and its practice. They are the very heart of the Buddha-Dhamma. It is not enough to know and admire the Dhamma; it must be practised in daily life, for the difficulty of knowing what is right is nothing compared to the difficulty of putting it into practice. We really know something only when we do it repeatedly, when we make it part of our nature. The practical side of the Dhamma is the threefold training in morality, concentration, and wisdom, which collectively constitute the Noble Eightfold Path, the "middle way" discovered by the Blessed One for the realization of Nibbāna.

Monastics and laypeople alike tread the same path. Both start from the same foundation, right understanding; both pursue the same goal, Nibbāna. The only difference lies in the degree of commitment to the practice and the pace of progress. But whether as a layperson or as a monk, the systematic practice of the Eightfold Path will foster the growth of the wholesome qualities leading to liberation—generosity, goodwill, and wisdom. As these qualities gradually reach maturity, they will weaken and finally snap the fetters of greed, hatred, and delusion which have held us for so long in bondage to the round of rebirth and suffering.

2. Benefits of Right Understanding

1. Right understanding is the foundation for developing a proper sense of values, so sorely lacking in our age. Without right understanding our vision is dimmed and the way is lost; all our efforts will be misguided and misdirected, all our plans for individual and social development must flounder and fail. Such plans will have to be based on the Eightfold Path with its emphasis on self-effort, self-control, and respect for the individual.

When wrong views prevail we will operate with a perverted sense of values: we will fling ourselves into the blind pursuit of wealth, power, and possessions; we will be obsessed by the urge to conquer and dominate; we will pine for ruthless revenge; we will dumbly conform to social conventions and norms. Right views will point us towards an enlightened sense of values: towards detachment and kindness; towards generosity of spirit and selfless service to others; towards the pursuit of wisdom and understanding. The confusion and moral lunacy now prevalent in the world can be eased, if not eliminated, if the path of the Buddha is followed. Right livelihood and right action, for instance, can help us avoid the conflicts that result from a wrong way of life and wrong action, thereby enabling a society to live in peace and harmony.

Although in the affluent countries of the West people now enjoy high standards of goods and services, the inward quality of their lives does not bear evidence of a corresponding level of improvement. The reason for the poverty of their interior life is the neglect of spiritual values. When materialism erodes the higher spiritual dimension of life, a plunge into moral nihilism is bound to follow. We see this in the alarming statistics characteristic of materialist society: in the increased rate of suicide, in the explosion of crime, in the proliferation of sexual offenses, alcoholism, and drug abuse. This shows that a one-sided stress on material development in a pleasure-seeking society is ultimately self-destructive, like a piece of iron that is devoured by the rust arising from within itself. Even knowledge and discipline on their own are not adequate, for without moral ideals they may turn a society into nothing more than a mass-scale workshop or military camp. It is only the cultivation of a proper sense of values that can make society cultured and civilized in the true meaning of those terms.

2. Having right understanding will enable us to recognize that worldly values are man-made and relative. These false worldly values lead people astray and make them suffer in vain. A Buddha teaches authentic values, real values, values that are grounded in timeless truth. A Buddha first realizes for himself the true nature of life, then he reveals to blind worldlings the Dhamma, the eternal law of righteousness and truth. This Dhamma includes the Four Noble Truths and the principles of kamma and rebirth. Any values that deviate from these principles, no matter how widely they may be accepted as the common norm, are worthless and deceptive. While those whose minds are shrouded in wrong views will be deceived by them, one with right view will realize their hollowness at once.

3. Seeing that life involves incessant change and that it is subject to many forms of suffering, one with right understanding learns to live simply and to regulate desire. A wise and virtuous person is moderate in his desires and follows the middle way in all matters. Understanding the close connection between craving and suffering, he will realize the importance of holding desire in check by simple living. One with right understanding is aware that real happiness is an inward state—a quality of the mind—and should therefore be sought inwardly. Happiness is independent of external things, though of course a certain degree of material security is necessary as a basis for inner development.

We require only four basic kinds of physical sustenance: wholesome food, clothing, shelter, and medicine. Complementary to these, we have four mental needs: right knowledge, virtue, guarding the doors of the senses, and meditation. These are the two sets of basic requisites for leading a lofty life. Living simply, without superfluous possessions and

Benefits of Right Understanding

entanglements, leads to contentment and peace of mind, releasing time and energy to pursue higher virtues and values. It is pride and vanity that keep us tied to false goals, and the smaller the mind, the greater is the pride.

4. Buddhism upholds the objectivity of moral values, for its ethics is based on the law of cause and effect in the moral sphere, and this law, like the physical law of gravity, is an unvarying truth valid for all time. Good deeds and bad deeds will produce their respective pleasant and painful fruits regardless of the views and wishes of the people who engage in them. Recognizing the objectivity of the moral law and the undeviating connection between deeds and their results, a person with right view will abstain from wrong actions and adhere to the standards of wholesome conduct embodied in the Five Precepts of virtuous conduct (discussed below).

5. As instability is inherent in life, the most unexpected things can happen. Therefore the wise Buddhist recognizes the need to control his feelings. When calamity comes, we must face it calmly, without lamenting or falling into despair. The ability to remain equanimous amidst the fluctuations of fortune is a benefit of right understanding. We should understand that everything that happens to us happens because of causes and conditions for which we are ultimately responsible. Similarly, as we obtain some degree of emotional control, we will be able to discard irrational fears and worries. The seeming injustices of life, grievances, emotional maladjustments, etc., are all explained fully and rationally by the law of kamma and rebirth. By understanding this law, we will see that, in the final analysis, we are the architects of our own destiny.

6. A further fruit of right understanding is the ability to look at people, things, and events objectively, stripped bare

of likes and dislikes, of bias and prejudice. This capacity for objectivity, a sign of true mental maturity, will issue in clearer thinking, saner living, a marked reduction of susceptibility to the pernicious influence of the mass media, and an improvement in inter-personal relationships.

7. One with right understanding will be able to think for himself. He is able to make up his own mind, to form his own opinions, to face life's difficulties armed with the principles of reality taught by the Buddha. The true Buddhist will not be a moral and intellectual coward, but will be prepared to stand alone regardless of what others say or think. Of course, he will seek advice when necessary, but he will make his own decisions and have the courage of his convictions.

8. Right understanding will give us a purpose for living. A lay Buddhist must learn to live purposefully, with a worthy aim—both an immediate aim and an ultimate aim, the one fitting harmoniously into the other. To be truly happy we require a simple but sound philosophy of life. Philosophy is the keen desire to understand the nature of man and our destiny in the universe. It gives life a sense of direction and meaning. Without one, we either dream our way through life or muddle through life. A clear-cut philosophy makes life meaningful and fruitful, enabling us to live in harmony with our fellows and with the natural environment.

3. A Life Plan

To make the best use of our human potential, we need not only a practical aim in life, but a life plan for achieving that aim. The preceding two sections of this essay show the groundwork for developing a proper sense of values, the values essential for gaining happiness, success, and security within

A Life Plan

the mundane life and for progressing towards the ultimate goal of the Buddhist path, Nibbāna. While we walk along the path to liberation, as laypeople we have to live in the world, and our immediate objective will be to make our life in the world both a means to worldly success and a stepping-stone to final liberation.

To accomplish this, we must organize our life within the framework of the Noble Eightfold Path. We can best realize our immediate aims by drawing up an individual life plan in keeping with our powers and circumstances. This life plan must be realistic. It must envisage a realistic development of our innate potential, steering us towards the fullest actualization of our possibilities.

At the start, we require an honest understanding of ourselves. It is pointless to devise a workable life plan on the foundation stone of grandiose delusions about our character and abilities. The more we find out about ourselves, by self-observation and self-examination, the better will be our chances of self-improvement. We should ask ourselves how far and to what degree we are generous, kind, even-tempered, considerate, honest, sober in morals, truthful, diligent, energetic, industrious, cautious, patient, tolerant, and tactful. These are the qualities of a well-developed Buddhist, the qualities we ourselves should emulate.

We need to improve ourselves wherever we are weak. A little practice everyday is all that is necessary. We should remember that the more often an action is performed, the easier it becomes for us to perform it in the future and the stronger becomes the tendency to do it again and again until it becomes a habit, an ingrained part of our character.

Our life plan should cover all the main areas of a normal householder's life, including occupation, marriage, the procreation and raising of children, retirement, old age and death. The happiness of lay life consists in finding out exactly what one can do and doing it well. A clear mental picture of a practical aim in life and a realistic sketch of the steps needed to achieve that aim will help guide us to the fulfilment of our ideal. We tend to become what we really want to be, provided we act realistically and effectively to realize our aim.

4. Obstacles

The following five states are likely to prevent or block the success of our efforts to lead the upright life of a Buddhist lay follower. They are called by the Buddha the five mental hindrances (*pañcanīvaraṇa*) because they close the doors to both spiritual and worldly progress. Although the Buddha originally taught them as the main obstacles to meditation, with a little reflection we can see that they are equally detrimental to success in our mundane undertakings.

1. The first of the five hindrances is *sensual craving*, obsessive hankering for possessions or for the gratification of the senses. While the lay Buddhist will seek wealth and possessions as an integral part of mundane happiness, he will also be aware of the limits to be observed in their pursuit. He will recognize that if one obtains wealth and position by unjust means, or becomes excessively attached to them, they will become a source of misery and despair rather than of joy and contentment. Money alone cannot solve all our problems. Many people never learn this, and spend their time and energy accumulating wealth and the so-called "good things" it can buy. But in fact, the more they acquire the more they want. Such people can never find happiness. A lay Buddhist must be moderate in all things. Extreme desires—for riches, the enjoyment of sex, liquor, the ostentatious dis-

play of one's success—are sure signs of internal insecurity, things to be avoided.

2. *Ill will* or hatred, the second hindrance, is the emotional opposite of desire, yet it is an equally potent obstacle to personal development. Because we are attracted to desirable things, we are repelled by what is undesirable. Like and dislike are the two forces that delude the world, leading people astray into conflict and confusion and drenching the earth with blood. Both are born of ignorance. Desire colours everything in tinsel and drives us to acquire what we want. Hatred colours everything black and drives us to destroy what we suspect is inimical to our interests. The best way to overcome hatred is by cultivating lovingkindness, explained later in this essay.

3. *Indolence and mental inertia* is the next hindrance, the obstacle to strenuous effort. The lazy person is not inclined to strive for correct understanding or high standards of conduct. He is a drifter or a dreamer, easy prey to the thieves of craving and hatred.

4. *Restlessness and worry* are twin hindrances very much in evidence today. Restlessness is manifest in the agitation, impatience, thirst for excitement, and unsettled character of our daily existence. Worry is the guilt and remorse that one feels when one broods sadly or regretfully over an evil deed that has been done or a good deed left undone. The best remedy for a lapse or transgression already committed is to decide never to repeat it; the best remedy for neglecting to do good is to do it without delay.

5. The last hindrance is *doubt*. Doubt is the inability to decide, the lack of resolution that prevents one from making a firm commitment to higher ideals and from pursuing the good with a steady will.

These five hindrances are great handicaps to one's progress. They deprive the mind of understanding and happiness and cause much unnecessary suffering. By cultivating the five cardinal virtues—confidence, energy, mindfulness, concentration, and wisdom—and by constant effort one can reduce their harmful influence.

5. Relaxation

Modern life is full of stress and strain. Therefore relaxation is a necessary ingredient of happiness. By understanding the causes of stress and by regulating these causes, we can live calmly even in the midst of strenuous activity.

Hard work without tension never killed anyone. Why is it then that some people always work anxiously and feverishly? Generally, such a person is driven by craving, by intense desire. He wants to achieve his goal so eagerly, with such avidity, that he simply cannot rest until he gets it; or he is so fearful of losing something he prizes that he cannot relax and enjoy the present moment; or he is driven by resentment against those who obstruct his thirst; or he is constantly hankering after power, position, and prestige on account of some irrational need to prove his worth to himself and others.

If a person wants to avoid stress and strain, then he will have to train his mind to view everything he encounters—persons, objects, events, and experiences—realistically, as transient phenomena, dependently arisen through conditions. He should reflect upon them in terms of the three characteristics—as impermanent, unsatisfactory, and without a self. Doing so will help to reduce the investment of self-concern in these phenomena, and thereby will reduce the craving and attachment for them. He should also avoid anger, anxiety, and pride—the thoughts of "me" and "mine"—since such emotions are productive of stress and strain. When one adopts this attitude to life, one will discover greater detachment, deeper calm, more durable peace of heart even amidst the same situations that previously produced nothing but stress and worry. The key to managing stress is through the disciplining and mastery of the mind.

One can also reduce stress by forming good work habits. One should confine oneself to doing one thing at a time, since attempts to juggle multiple tasks only lead to poor results in all of them. One should keep work and leisure separate. One should work in a relaxed frame of mind, repeatedly reminding oneself during the course of the day that one can accomplish more work and better work if one works calmly and intersperses one's routine with breaks.

The following additional disciplines will also be helpful in combatting stress and tension:

1. Keeping the Five Precepts conscientiously. The feeling of guilt increases stress. By observing the precepts, a person leads a blameless life and thereby enjoys freedom from the nagging sense of guilt that harasses one who violates the basic rules of morality. A guilty conscience is a vexing companion during the day, an uncomfortable bed-fellow at night.

2. Sense control. The mind is constantly attracted to pleasant sense objects and repelled by unpleasant objects. Wandering recklessly among the objective fields, it becomes scattered and distraught. By guarding the sense doors, this wasteful agitation is checked. The mind becomes calm and settled, and as a result one experiences an unblemished happiness.

3. Meditation. Meditation, or *bhāvanā*, purifies the mind.

As the mind is gradually cleansed, one can see with greater clarity the true nature of life. One then becomes increasingly detached from worldly things and develops an equanimity that cannot be shaken by the fluctuations of fortune.

4. Cultivating the four sublime attitudes. The four sublime attitudes (*brahmavihāra*) are lovingkindness, compassion, altruistic joy, and equanimity. These are enlightened emotions that reduce the stress and strain of daily life, improve interpersonal relationships at home and in the workplace, promote racial accord and amity, help in the development of an even mind, and increase calm and inner peace.

5. One final piece of practical advice: Time, energy, and funds are limited, while wants are unlimited. Therefore a person must have a sense of priorities. A lay Buddhist, in particular, must be able to discriminate: to know what is really essential to a wholesome life; what is desirable but not urgent; what is trivial and dispensable; and what is detrimental. Having made these distinctions, one must pursue what ranks high in the scale of priorities and eschew what ranks low. This will enable one to avoid unnecessary waste and worry, and help to promote balanced, frugal living.

6. Observing the Five Precepts

The minimal code of ethics followed by a lay Buddhist is the Five Precepts of virtue (*pañcasīla*). These precepts are moral rules voluntarily undertaken to promote the purity of one's own conduct and to avoid causing harm and suffering to others. Evil conduct is harmful to oneself and others and strengthens the defilements of greed, hatred, and delusion. To engage in unwholesome activity is not merely a matter of free choice: it is a violation of the cosmic moral law entailing inevitable suffering both in this life and in future existences. The opposite of evil conduct is virtue (*sīla*). Virtue involves the avoidance of immoral deeds by voluntarily accepting ethical principles of restraint. Virtuous action springs from the three wholesome roots of non-attachment, goodwill, and wisdom. By undertaking moral precepts one pledges to regulate one's conduct in accordance with these three virtuous qualities.

The Five Precepts are as follows:

1. To abstain from killing living beings;
2. To abstain from taking what is not given, i.e. from stealing;
3. To abstain from sexual misconduct;
4. To abstain from false speech;
5. To abstain from intoxicants and harmful drugs.

Following the Five Precepts also implies shunning the five kinds of occupation forbidden to a lay Buddhist: trading in arms, in human beings (i.e. including slavery and prostitution), in flesh (i.e. breeding animals for slaughter), in intoxicants, and in poisons.

Virtue, though formulated negatively in the precepts, is not a mere negative state. To the contrary, it is most decidedly a powerful mental achievement. To observe the precepts conscientiously in one's daily life brings a simultaneous growth in mental purity, skilfulness, and wisdom. Refraining from killing, for example, increases compassion and lovingkindness for all living beings, two of the "sublime attitudes" extolled by the Buddha. Honesty gives courage, generosity, and love of justice. Sexual restraint results in physical strength, vitality, and keenness of the senses. Truthfulness makes for uprightness. Avoiding intoxicants and stupefying drugs promotes clarity of mind. Finally, mindfulness is essential to observing all the precepts, and one's constant effort to maintain the precepts in turn issues in an increase in the clarity of mindfulness.

The habitual practice of the Five Precepts leads to increased self-control and strength of character. The mind that succeeds in controlling desire, even to a slight degree, gains in power. Desire is a force every bit as real as electricity. When desire is uncontrolled, allowed to run riot, it expends itself in the pursuit of things that are harmful to oneself and others. The Buddha's teaching, far from encouraging the proliferation of desire, counsels us in the methods by which we may harness, divert, and sublimate the powerful force of desire and use it for worthy ends.

Virtue is the first stage in the development of the Noble Eightfold Path; as explained above, it comprises the path factors of Right Speech, Right Action, and Right Livelihood. The energy conserved by virtue is then used for the practice of the second stage, concentration of mind, which in turn is the soil for the growth of wisdom.

The observance of the Five Precepts is a voluntary act which each individual must take up on his or her own initiative. The Buddha did not formulate the precepts as commandments, nor did he threaten anyone with punishment for violating them. However, this much has to be said: The Buddha perfectly understood the workings of the universe, and he proclaimed the inviolable moral law of cause and effect: good deeds beget pleasant fruits, evil deeds beget painful fruits. The Five Precepts are the guidelines the Buddha has bequeathed us to steer us away from evil conduct and towards the lines of conduct that will prove most beneficial for ourselves and others. When we mould our actions by the Five Precepts, we are acting in accordance with the Dhamma, avoiding future misery and building up protection and happiness for ourselves and others both here and in the hereafter. Thus the closer we live to the Five Precepts, the greater will be the blessing power of our lives.

7. Controlling the Emotions

An emotion is a state of deep feeling, an "inward stirring" which can act as a motivation for action. Emotions are often associated with the instincts, the inborn tendencies to act in specific ways in specific situations. Human beings are conditioned to a very great extent by their emotions, by their likes and dislikes. Too often their emotions are biased by self-interest and egotism, even to the extent that they overwhelm sense and reason, compelling us to act in ways that, in saner moments, we regard with dismay.

Emotions generally arise in response to the spontaneous evaluation of perceptions. A person evaluates his or her percepts—of another person, an object, a situation—as desirable or undesirable, as helpful or as threatening. On the basis of this evaluation an emotion will arise in response to the situation: desire for those things positively evaluated, aversion or fear towards those things seen in a negative light. Emotions may be harmful, such as lust, anger, and fear, or wholesome, such as sympathy and compassion. While desire and aversion are the prototypes of the unwholesome emotions, lovingkindness and compassion are outstanding examples of emotions that ennoble us and elevate human nature.

People vary widely in their emotional development and in the range and strength of their emotions. While one person is passionate and impulsive, another is cool and reflective; while one is quick to anger, another is patient; while one is emotionally impassive, another is capable of running through a wide range of emotions in less time than a finger snap. One important reason for these differences is that each individual brings along a different kammic inheritance of tendencies and character traits from previous lives. Whether emotions are repressed or expressed, indulged in or sublimated, depends on a combination of factors: innate temperament, family background, and the ethos and traditions of the larger society.

We cannot grow in the Dhamma or find happiness without some degree of emotional control. A person who easily gets angry spoils his own happiness and disturbs the peace of mind of others as well. Instinctive emotions are the raw material of character. If an instinctive impulse is misdirected or repressed, much harm and suffering may ensue. But if the energy that is normally channeled into this emotion is redirected towards a worthy object, the force of the emotion will be sublimated in a way that results in great benefit to oneself and to the community. For the Buddhist, the worthiest of all ideals is the attainment of Nibbāna; hence it is the quest for this ideal that has the capacity to absorb and transform our emotional life. Such a noble ideal has the power of evoking and harmonizing all our emotional energies so that they guide us towards the realization of our ultimate good.

Without deliberate effort, emotions will not be under the direct control of the will. The Buddhist training aims at mastering the emotions. The first step in gaining such mastery is the observance of the Five Precepts. Practising the precepts in everyday life will help us to control the grosser forms of craving and emotion. The next step is to train the mind to control the emotions just as they begin to arise. This is accomplished by mindfulness: by objectively watching, with close attention, the emotions that arise and swiftly ascribing a name to them, a mental label thus: "mind with lust," "mind with anger," "mind with jealousy," "mind with sorrow," etc. Once we have named the emotion, we are then in a better position to let it go, without being swept away by it. The moment one calmly registers the fact that one is angry—when one is *aware* of the fact that a mind with anger has arisen—one then ceases to be angry. A mind that is occupied with the wholesome thought of mindful awareness has no scope within it simultaneously for an unwholesome thought of anger.

This same procedure should be adopted with any other harmful emotion that arises. At the start it may prove helpful if, during the course of the day, one mentally repeats to oneself a formula such as: "What am I feeling now?" or "What am I thinking now?" and immediately answers the question thus: "I am feeling angry," or "I am feeling jealous," etc. We should also investigate, even later, when and why anger—or any other adverse emotion—overwhelmed us *then*, and thus avoid such situations and responses in the future.

By patient and persistent practice we can gradually gain control over our harmful emotions. The discipline and effort involved is worthwhile, for it will bring greater harmony internally—in one's own mind—and externally, in one's relations with others. The key to such control is firm adherence to the basic precepts of morality and, above all, mindfulness of one's own thoughts and emotions.

8. Beware of Bias and Propaganda

Buddhism teaches the need for clear thinking, self-control, self-help, and meditation. Although each human being is endowed with a mind, very few of us use that mind to think for ourselves. The great majority of people today allow others to do their thinking for them.

The mind absorbs a great deal of poison from the outer environment by continuous exposure to suggestions from others. This mental passivity has become especially baneful with the development of the mass media. Radio, television, and newspapers, pulp journals and tabloids, blare their messages at us every minute of the day, and their power of penetration is reinforced by the ingrained human disposition to accept what we are told and to comply with what we are urged to do. Bombarded left and right by ten thousand inducements, we no longer think our own thoughts, feel our own emotions, or initiate our own actions; instead, we think as others want us to think, feel as others want us to feel, act in ways that will win the approval of our peers and superiors. The pull of the crowd has become irresistible.

Every time we open a newspaper, turn on the radio, or sit down before the television set, we are immediately subjected to propaganda, advertising, and subtle social suggestions. This is done daily, deliberately and systematically. All these media are teaching us to suspend our capacity for thought, or if we are to think at all, to think as they would like us to think. Newspapers, for instance, seek to command assent not only by their editorials and opinion columns, but by their layout, language, and lines of emphasis.

Those who exploit the media in this manner are generally small but powerful groups: the owners and sponsors of the media, advertising agencies, the masters of commerce. Such people are motivated primarily by self-interest, greed for wealth and power, a sense of self-importance. Often they play dominant roles in various walks of life, including politics, business, law, medicine, and education. Among the general public the role of reason tends to be subordinate to that of emotion, while mental inertia and indifference make the conquest of reason easier. Hence, by shaping public opinion through the manipulation of the media, a small minority is able to control the majority.

Those who comprise this small but powerful minority all have something to sell. Commercial advertisements make us want more and more goods that bring us no real happiness, no real peace of mind. We are told that our felicity depends on having a radio, television, video player, stereo set, and computer games. Yet, however much we deck ourselves with all these instruments of diversion, we still feel our lives painfully lacking.

The speed, power, and efficiency of all these technological and social developments within a purely materialistic society such as ours has led to a rising incidence of stress disease and mental breakdown. Those who do not crack under pressure find other escape routes, such as drugs, alcohol, and psychotic cults, while for those who cannot cope at all there remains the last resort: suicide, which has reached alarming proportions in our midst.

How then is a Buddhist to protect himself or herself from the baneful influences to which we are everywhere exposed in the modern world? As lay Buddhists we should always adopt a critical attitude towards the written and spoken word and should always apply mindfulness to protect ourselves from being emotionally swayed by those who seek to win our favour. We should stand back from the topic under review and examine it objectively from all angles. Only after appraising the alternatives should we arrive at a decision or evaluation.

When we hear a particular opinion being voiced, we should make an effort to find out who the writer or speaker is, what interests he or she represents, including political affiliations, religious leanings, and social background. We should also never forget that there are at least two sides to any issue, and that we are more likely to arrive at a correct stand if we first give unbiased consideration to both sides. Before arriving at a conclusion, one should gather all the relevant facts, maintain a calm mind free from emotional excitation, and prevent oneself from being swayed by preferences and anger, praise and blame. The same principle of objective thinking should also be applied to other matters in everyday life.

If we properly understand the working of kamma and rebirth, we will recognize that no one can be alike, and thus we will also avoid drawing comparisons; for this is a world of comparisons as well as of propaganda. The only meaningful comparison that one should make is between the person that one was a month ago, a year ago, or a decade ago, and the person that one is now: physically, intellectually, morally, and financially. If there has been no improvement, or insufficient improvement, one should inquire why this is so and remedy one's deficiencies without delay. If this annual stocktaking is done regularly, it will be most beneficial. Putting aside pride and prejudice, revising one's values and outlook, one will then lead a simpler, saner, and happier life.

9. A Happy Family Life

For the adult it is natural to love one person of the opposite sex. The lay Buddhist will recognize that there is nothing "sinful" or shameful in sex, and hence will not suffer from a guilt complex over sexual desire. At the same time he or she will be aware that sexual desire, like any other form of desire, must be regulated and controlled to avoid harm to oneself and to others.

In a successful marriage the contracting parties must realize that love is a sentiment far wider than sexual attraction. If one person really loves another, he or she has to learn to give without expecting anything in return. Only in this way can the problem of sex be solved satisfactorily. Further, the would-be partners should ask themselves, "What do I expect of my partner?" and should find out objectively to what extent the prospective partner has the requisite qualities. One might enlist the help of a trustworthy, balanced friend who has known the would-be partner for some time and might be in a better position to offer a correct evaluation. There are obvious dangers in being one's own marriage broker. Too often one is inclined to endow the would-be partner with qualities and virtues that she (or he) clearly lacks in the eyes of the unbiased observer. This danger has to be frankly acknowledged, for disillusionment might otherwise set in sooner or later, and then the stage is set for marital discontent and misery.

No doubt, in married life sex is important, but it must be kept in its proper place, as an expression of marital love. Sex is by no means the sole concern of married life; only when it is subordinated to personal love and affection does sexuality provide a truly satisfying emotional experience. Above and beyond sexual compatibility, a happy marriage calls for mutual understanding and adjustments, for sacrifices and selflessness, for tolerance and patience. Married life becomes truly a blessing rather than a curse when it is viewed as a partnership of two persons who are committed to think more of the partnership than they do of themselves, who are ready to make the mutual effort necessary to attain harmony and contentment.

Most married couples hope to have children. Children differ, for each brings his or her own kammic inheritance from many past lives, a kammic inheritance that includes potential tendencies that set the general tone and trend of the child's character. This fact indicates both the responsibilities and the limitations of the parents in the upbringing of their children.

The child spends most of the formative years of his or her life at home, and early in life learns to follow by imitation the values and lifestyle of the parents. Schools and other influential agencies cannot supplant or replace the parents. Buddhist parents should recognize their solemn obligation to serve as models for their children. They should therefore regularly observe the Five Precepts and show their children by example that the Dhamma yet lives and rules their daily lives. Parents must be aware that the child has immense potentials for both good and evil, and thus must fulfil their responsibility to help the child to develop his or her potential for good and to check the potential for evil. It is only if parents bestow their loving care and attention on their child that the child will be able to satisfy the hopes and aspirations of the parents.

The Buddha has advised parents to guide their children, to supply their needs, to see to their education, to give them in marriage at the proper time, and to attend to all other aspects of their well-being. Unfortunately, however, many parents today do not discharge these duties, with the result that too often children go astray. Responsible Buddhist parents must be prepared to forgo their own pleasure in order

A Happy Family Life

to attend to the upbringing of their children. They must realize that the home influence is ultimately what matters most in forming the child's character, outweighing all other outside influences to which the child may be exposed. In areas where the parents lack adequate expertise, they should be prepared to consult a non-technical manual on proper child rearing.

The first five years of a child's life are the most crucial in the formation of his or her character, and it is at this stage that they are most susceptible to the influence of the parents. Thereafter the needs of the child change, and will continue to change radically at different stages of development. Parents should remember this and meet the new needs as they arise.

In the early years three factors are essential for balanced and wholesome growth: parental love and affection; a stable home environment; and scope for creative activity and personal initiative. Young children learn largely by imitation. If parents show emotional maturity, avoid quarrels, respect and trust each other, and do likewise with their children, then the children will develop characters that are sound both morally and psychologically. When the child is brought up with love and understanding, with insight into his or her changing needs, nourished with high ideals and lofty aspirations, then he or she will have a secure foundation upon which to build a character and a future. In this way the very first steps along the Buddha's path will have been well planted.

Adolescence is a period of stress and strain, when children may be inclined to rebel against parental authority. It is therefore at this stage that the greatest love and understanding are called for. In adolescence, as the sexual instinct awakens, sensible Buddhist parents should be capable of guiding their children and helping them to adjust to the changes taking place in their bodies and their lives. When children ask their parents questions about sex, the parents should be ready to answer them calmly and briefly in a matter-of-fact way, just as they would answer any other question. If parents are unable to tell the adolescent children the facts of life in an unselfconscious manner they might give them a suitable book to enable them to instruct themselves about the subject. Above all, in this age of sexually provocative entertainment, irresponsible promiscuity, and an exploding AIDS epidemic, withholding vital information is not a means of protecting the youngster but of exposing him or her to danger.

When parental control, supervision, and proper guidance are lacking, the children often incline to delinquency and drugs. Parents should therefore take greater interest in their children, should spend more time with them, should know how they use their leisure, and should make the acquaintance of their friends. Real problem children are few; it is only problem parents who are many.

As the child reaches maturity it is the duty of the parents to help him wisely choose a suitable career as well as a mate, but the child's wishes in these spheres have to be respected. To order the young person about as if he or she were still a child is only to invite trouble.

Since we live in a world of keen competition in many areas of life, wise Buddhist parents will limit the size of their family in order to give their children the best. In developing countries like Sri Lanka, where the rate of reproduction is generally higher than the rate of production of real wealth, this is a necessary measure to eliminate poverty, especially among the working classes in both town and countryside, whose families are generally large with many dependants.

A Happy Family Life

Buddhism is not opposed to population control, except by means of abortion, and with the world's resources dwindling today under dense population pressure, Buddhist parents should recognize the need for family limitation to ensure the best for the children.

In a country like Sri Lanka it is the duty of the state to popularize family limitation by making freely available safe, effective, and inexpensive methods of birth control. Production that is centred on the population at large—rather than on enhancing the wealth of a privileged few—using appropriate technology, with just distribution of resources and extensive family planning, will increase real wealth and help to improve the quality of life of the masses, provided they also cultivate a wise sense of values. Otherwise they will always remain poor.

The moral and spiritual edification of the children should accompany their physical and emotional development. As they grow up, parents should teach them the essentials of the Buddha-Dhamma, using simple language and everyday examples. They should explain the working of the moral law of kamma and rebirth, should instruct them in the proper rules of conduct, and should clarify the reasons for practising virtue in daily life. Furthermore, in a Buddhist country children should be regularly taken to the temple, especially on quiet days. They should be enrolled in Dhamma school if such is available, and should be encouraged to ask their questions and discuss their problems with wise and virtuous bhikkhus. The Dhamma, after all, is intended to guide us in how to live this very life we are leading now. It is the art of happiness here and now, and the path to deliverance in the hereafter.

Materialism is steadily eroding traditional values, moral,

spiritual, and social. The influence of materialism now reaches even the remote villages, the ancient strongholds of the Buddhist way of life. But young people who have been rightly brought up by Buddhist parents to discover the value of the Dhamma for themselves are unlikely to be led astray.

10. The Practice of Benevolence

The desire to do good, to bring about the happiness and well-being of others, is effectively cultivated in Buddhism by the systematic practice of the four "sublime attitudes" (*brahmavihāra*): lovingkindness (*mettā*), compassion (*karuṇā*), altruistic joy (*muditā*), and equanimity (*upekkhā*). By cultivating these qualities a Buddhist can gradually remove the mental defilements such as hatred, cruelty, and envy, and bring into being the most exalted virtues. The sublime attitudes elevate human beings to a divine-like stature; they break the barriers that separate individuals and groups; they build bridges more solid than those constructed of stone and steel.

1. *Mettā* is goodwill, lovingkindness, universal love; a feeling of friendliness and heartfelt concern for all living beings, human or non-human, in all situations. The chief mark of *mettā* is a benevolent attitude: a keen desire to promote the welfare of others. *Mettā* subdues the vice of hatred in all its varied shades: anger, ill-will, aversion, and resentment. The Buddha said:

> Hatreds do not cease through hatreds
> Anywhere at anytime.
> Through love alone do they cease:
> This is an eternal law.

(Dhp. v. 5)

This stanza is of special significance to us in this nuclear era when the most appalling destructiveness has erupted all over the globe. Peace will never be achieved by meeting force with force, bombs with bombs, violence with retaliation. *Mettā* or lovingkindness is the only effective answer to violence and destructiveness, whether by conventional weapons or nuclear missiles.

2. *Karuṇā* is the attitude conveyed by such terms as compassion, sympathy, pity, and mercy. Its basic characteristic is sympathy for all who suffer, and it arouses a desire to relieve or remove the pain and suffering of others. *Karuṇā* helps to eliminate callousness and indifference to others' woes. It is the direct antidote to cruelty, another vice common in the world today. It is compassion that prompts one to serve others selflessly, expecting nothing, not even gratitude, in return.

3. *Muditā* is altruistic joy, appreciative joy: the desire to see others rejoicing in their happiness, the ability to share the happiness and success of others. This attitude is the complement of *karuṇā*: while *karuṇā* shares the sorrow of others, *muditā* shares their joy. *Muditā* is the direct antidote to envy. Envy arises over the good fortune of others: it resents those who achieve position, prestige, power, and success. But one who practises *muditā* will not only be happy when others do well, but will try to promote their progress and welfare. Hence this attitude is of vital importance for achieving social concord and peace.

4. *Upekkhā*, the last of the four sublime attitudes, is equanimity. *Upekkhā* establishes an even or balanced mind in an unbalanced world with fluctuating fortunes and circumstances: gain and loss, fame and ill-repute, praise and blame, pleasure and pain. *Upekkhā* also looks upon all beings impartially, as

heirs to the results of their own actions, without attachment or aversion. *Upekkhā* is the serene neutrality of the one who knows.

The constant, methodical, and deliberate cultivation of these sublime virtues in everyday life transforms the attitudes and outlook of the practitioner. They should be the foundation of all Buddhist social action, as well as of individual and collective peace and harmony. Buddhist social welfare work may take many forms, but what is most essential is the spirit in which it is performed. This spirit should be marked by the subordination of the private good to the good of the whole. For Buddhist social work to be of real value, action should spring from genuine love, sympathy, and understanding for one's fellow humans, guided by knowledge and training. Welfare work should be the perfect expression of compassion, untouched by condescension, washed clean of pride—even of the pride of doing good. It should be a sheer manifestation of the brotherhood of all human beings.

The four sublime attitudes should be diligently cultivated with unremitting effort by every true follower of the Master. These qualities never become obsolete. They convey a universal message which transforms us into universal human beings.

11. Freeing the Mind

Mind occupies the pre-eminent place in Buddhism, for everything that one says or does first arises in the mind as a thought. To have a well-trained mind is indeed to possess a treasure. When a person trains the mind, turns inward to examine and cleanse his own mind, he will find therein a vast storehouse of happiness. Real happiness is a quality of the mind which has to be sought and found in the mind. The Buddha teaches that non-attachment to worldly pleasures is a greater happiness than the enjoyment of worldly pleasures. Nibbāna is the highest happiness, the happiness of relief from suffering and from repeated birth, and this happiness is only to be attained by freeing the mind from its defilements.

The misguided worldling thinks otherwise. In his view the enjoyment of sensual pleasures is the only real happiness. He forgets, however, that sensual happiness arises merely from the gratification of desire, and thus that this happiness must fade when the desired object is obtained. Nor will the multiplication of desires make sensual pleasure permanent, for there is no permanence in the passing. The pursuit of sensual pleasures ends only in restlessness and dissatisfaction.

The aim of Buddhist mental culture is to gain direct intuitive knowledge of the real nature of existence by systematic training of the mind through meditation. This practice issues in detachment and thus frees the mind from its delusions. Meditation leads the mind from the pain-laden things of the world to the sorrowless, transcendent state of deliverance, Nibbāna. The basic cause of rebirth and suffering is ignorance of the true nature of life. We consider what is passing, unsatisfactory, and empty to be permanent, a source of true happiness, and substantial. This delusion sustains the craving for more existence and leads to the accumulation of kamma. Meditation is designed to lead step-by-step to the dissolution of these delusions and thereby to freedom from the grip of craving.

There are two kinds of meditation recognized in Buddhism: the development of tranquillity (*samatha-bhāvanā*), which emphasizes concentration, and the development of insight (*vipassanā-bhāvanā*), which emphasizes wisdom. These two types of meditation respectively correspond to the second and third groups of the Noble Eightfold Path, the concentration group and the wisdom group. Concentration means one-pointedness of the mind, the ability to fix the mind on a single object to the exclusion of all else. Concentration is not an end in itself, but to be developed primarily because it is the basis for wisdom, the ability to see things exactly as they are. It is this wisdom that frees the mind from bondage.

To train the mind is not at all easy, for the mind has long been accustomed to flow in the channels of greed, hatred, and delusion; through ages we have relished sense pleasures, raged with anger, wallowed in torpor, fidgeted restlessly, and vacillated with doubt. Such habits are indeed difficult to break. Moreover, it is the very nature of the untrained mind to wander from one idea to another. Thus when the meditator sits down to begin the practice, strange thoughts may dance before his mind. To overcome these disturbances, the Buddha has taught five methods of expelling distracting thoughts:

1. Develop a good thought opposed to the distracting one; for example, develop a thought of lovingkindness to expel a thought of hatred.

2. Reflect on the evil consequences of distracting thoughts; for example, ill will or anger may lead to harsh words or an exchange of blows, to making enemies, or to something worse.

3. Turn the mind away from the disturbing thought and fix it on some beneficial idea or towards some useful activity.

4. Trace the cause of the uprisen evil thought and reflect on whether it will serve any useful purpose.

5. Struggle directly with the evil thought to crush it and subdue it.

At the outset meditation will be a continual effort to pull the mind back whenever it strays from the subject of meditation. It will seem impossible to focus the attention on the selected subject for more than a few seconds at a stretch. With continued practice, however, one will refine one's skills until one can keep the mind focused steadily and calmly on the chosen topic for increasingly longer periods. Then the practice becomes more engaging, more rewarding, and also less tiring. Eventually one's efforts will culminate in one-pointedness of mind, *samādhi*.

With the attainment of the one-pointed mind, the meditator turns this pure, steady, clear mind to the contemplation of existence itself. This marks the beginning of *vipassanā-bhāvanā*, the meditative development of insight. The meditator mindfully investigates his own compound of the "five aggregates." He sees that the body, or form, is made up of changing physical qualities, while mind itself consists of fleeting mental factors: feeling, perception, mental formations (intentions, emotions, thoughts, desires, etc.), and consciousness. He sees that these all occur in mutual dependence, all in a flow. There is no substantial self, no immortal soul within them to be called "I" or "mine." As the impermanence, the unsatisfactoriness, and the selfless nature of the five aggregates become manifest to the meditator, he realizes that nothing conditioned is worth clinging to; for everything conditioned is fleeting, and in the fleeting it is impossible to find stable happiness. This is *paññā*, wisdom, the third and final stage in the Noble Eightfold Path.

With the development of wisdom, ignorance ceases in all its forms and shades. Craving and kamma, the fuel for the flame of becoming, is exhausted, and no more fresh fuel is supplied. Hence the flame of existence burns out for lack of fuel. When such a person who has reached the goal passes away, he no longer takes rebirth in any realm of becoming. He has attained Nibbāna, the Deathless.

12. Mindfulness of Breathing

Mindfulness of breathing (*ānāpānasati*) is an excellent subject of meditation particularly useful to the busy layperson, as it can be practised safely by anyone, anywhere, at any time. To practise this type of meditation, one should first adopt a seated meditation posture. Those who can sit comfortably in full lotus or half-lotus posture may adopt those positions; those who find this difficult may assume any cross-legged sitting posture that enables them to hold upright the upper part of the body; those who find even this difficult may sit on a straight-backed chair. The torso should be held erect but not stiff; the hands should be placed one over the other on the lap; and (for those who sit in a chair) the feet should rest on the floor.

The meditator should then breathe calmly and naturally, mentally following the whole breath in and out without a break in attentiveness. At the outset one should simply breathe in and out without reflecting about it. One may fix the attention on the nostrils or upper lip, wherever the breath is felt most distinctly as one breathes in and out. There the attention should remain.

As one proceeds with the observation of the breath, one becomes more and more deeply concentrated upon it. One then feels light in body and mind, very calm and peaceful;

one may even feel as if one were floating in the air. When strong calm is established and the mind becomes one-pointed, one may then turn one's attention towards the development of insight (*vipassanā*), aiming to gain direct insight into the true nature of existence. This type of meditation, when successful, leads by stages to the realization of Nibbāna.

Apart from its ultimate benefits, mindfulness of breathing has an immediate value that can be seen in one's daily life. It promotes detachment and objectivity. It allows one the mental distance needed to arrive at wise decisions in the countless difficulties of daily life. Regular practice of this meditation brings increased concentration and self-control, improved mindfulness, and is also conducive to healthy and relaxed living.

13. Facing Death with Equanimity

Death is the only absolutely certain thing in life, yet how many of us plan for it and prepare ourselves adequately in advance to face it calmly? All human beings must die. The body disintegrates, breaks apart, and turns to ashes and dust. The only thing we own that remains with us beyond death is our kamma, our intentional deeds. Our deeds continue, bringing into being a new form of life until all craving is extinguished. We are born and evolve according to the quality of our kamma. Good deeds will produce a good rebirth, bad deeds a bad rebirth.

The materialistic view that a human being is merely a biological result of the union of sperm and ovum which utterly terminates in death is inadequate as a total explanation of human life. Nature and nurture, heredity and the environment, cannot by themselves explain, for example, why twins born of the same parents, physically almost identical, enjoying equal privileges, brought up in the same environment, often exhibit widely different characteristics, mental, moral, and emotional. Moreover, science would meet difficulties accounting for the existence of infant prodigies and the recollection of past lives, particularly by children.

A realistic Buddhist, knowing that death is inevitable, plans for it and trains himself to face it with equanimity. He also knows that the best way to plan for death is to lead a virtuous and upright life. Thus the devoted Buddhist regularly observes the Five Precepts, performs many kind and generous acts, and endeavours to lessen his greed and hate. The fact that one has led a blameless life will be an added solace and source of strength at death. The fear of death then loses its force and sting.

In preparing for death, a householder should fulfil his obligations to his family, to others, and to his religion. In practice, this means leaving behind a sufficient income for one's family, making out a proper last will, planning one's own funeral arrangements, and providing funds for the maintenance of virtuous and learned monks who observe the rules of discipline and who can preach the correct Dhamma.

The Buddha teaches his lay followers, as well as the monks and nuns, that they should often reflect on the inevitability of death: "Death is certain, life is uncertain" (*maraṇaṁ niyataṁ, jīvitaṁ aniyataṁ*). These words are a clarion call reminding us of the need to put our own house in order, morally and philosophically, without delay, and to face each day as if it were our last. The world of today would indeed be a happier and safer place to live if people the world over would only pay heed to this call.

14. The Good Buddhist

The preceding sections of this essay will help the Buddhist lay follower to understand, from a practical angle, the main points of the Buddha's teachings as they bear on the conduct of daily life. Constant practice of these principles will ensure that they are built into his character, enabling him to develop into a well-rounded human being, a centre of sanity in a confused world adrift in fashionable philosophies full of empty promises.

At the very minimum a lay follower of the Buddha must keep the Five Precepts, which enables him to develop virtue in regard to his bodily and verbal behaviour. But one should not stop with this. One who seeks the true perfection of happiness must also attend to the cultivation of the mind. One must be mindful of the arising of unwholesome states such as greed, anger, and delusion, and know how to deal with them effectively when they threaten to throw one off balance. One should proceed even further and attempt to cultivate the mind systematically through the practice of meditation for tranquillity and insight.

The society in which we live is a reflection of the minds of the human beings who have created that society. If our society has become corrupt, rife with immorality, and destructive of the higher potentials of human nature, that is because the people who comprise that society have allowed themselves to drift into corrupt and immoral states of mind. The quality of a society inevitably rests on the quality of the lives led by the persons who make up that society. One single individual may not be able to change the whole society for the better. But each one of us can, at any rate, transform the world of our own mind.

How is this to be done? By observing the Five Precepts flawlessly, by being as mindful as possible in everyday life, by cleansing the mind of its blemishes, by cultivating the four sublime states, by meditating energetically every day, by listening to discourses on the Dhamma and clarifying one's doubts about the teaching. By following these guidelines one is sure to reap their fruits: peace of mind, contentment, the absence of inner conflicts even in the midst of our confusing and chaotic world.

A good Buddhist should ever seek the opportunity to do deeds of mercy, kindness, and charity. He should be keen on helping those less fortunate than himself. When practising giving, however, one should give with discrimination, as the Buddha advises: *viceyya dānaṁ dātabbaṁ*. Thus the most needy will be benefited with the things they need most.

A good Buddhist should set apart a few minutes every day to review the day's happenings, and to see whether or not he has strayed from the Master's teachings. If so, he should inquire why he has done so in order to avoid a future repetition. Methodical reading on the Dhamma will also help one to put the whole of life into the right perspective. It is a useful habit to read daily an inspiring discourse of the Buddha, such as the Mahāmaṅgala Sutta, or to recite some verses of the Dhammapada and reflect for a few moments on their relevance to one's own life. Doing so will help one to forget one's trifling worries and troubles, to clarify one's thinking, and to recall the ultimate values and truths upon which one should build one's life.

The Buddha's teachings consist of virtue, concentration, and wisdom. Only with their practice will the Buddha-Dhamma flourish; when they are neglected, the Buddha-Dhamma will decline. This fact should always be remembered by those who are anxious to avert the decline and disappearance of the Sāsana. As religion withers the world over, more and more attention is paid to empty rites, rituals, and ceremonies, while little or no attention is paid to the actual practice of the principles of religion as they bear on real life. It is this, however, that matters most.

By following the above guidelines, a good Buddhist will grow in all aspects of the Dhamma. These guidelines will help to mould one's whole personality, to instil the true principles of the Dhamma into one's understanding, to train the emotions and to discipline the will. Doing so will conduce to the ultimate best interest of oneself, and help one to make one's life a blessing for others as well.

> May you and I and all other beings
> be well and happy.

About the Author

Robert Bogoda was born in 1918 in Colombo, the business capital of Sri Lanka. His secondary education was cut short by the sudden demise of his father, which compelled him to work at a modest job as a teacher. While engaged in teaching, he obtained by self study the B.Sc. (Econ.) and M.Sc. (Econ.) degrees from the University of London, specializing in Social Administration. Now retired, he pursues his interests in Buddhism and social welfare. The essay "A Simple Guide to Life" was written against this background.

Of related interest from The Wheel series

The Buddha's Words on Kamma
Trans. by Bhikkhua Ñāṇamoli (Wh 248/249)

Buddhism and Sex
M.O'C. Walshe (Wh 225)

The Buddhist Layman
R. Bogoda et al. (Wh 294/295)

Buddhist Reflections on Death
V.F. Gunaratna (Wh 102/103)

Dāna: The Practice of Giving
Edited by Bhikkhu Bodhi (Wh 367/369)

The Five Mental Hindrances
Nyanaponika Thera (Wh 26)

The Four Sublime States
Nyanaponika Thera (Wh 6)

Going for Refuge & Taking the Precepts
Bhikkhu Bodhi (Wh 282/284)

Lay Buddhist Practice
Bhikkhu Khantipālo (Wh 206/207)

Life's Highest Blessings
R.L. Soni (Wh 254/256)

Mettā: Philosophy & Practice of Universal Love
Acharya Buddharakkhita (Wh 365/366)

Muditā: Unselfish Joy
Nyanaponika Thera et al. (Wh 170)

One Foot in the World
Lily de Silva (Wh 337/338)

The Practice of Loving Kindness
Bhikkhu Ñāṇamoli (Wh 7)

The Roots of Good & Evil
Nyanaponika Thera (Wh 251/253)

The Scale of Good Deeds
Susan Elbaum Jootla (Wh 372)

For details see our latest catalogue

THE BUDDHIST PUBLICATION SOCIETY

The BPS is an approved charity dedicated to making known the Teaching of the Buddha, which has a vital message for people of all creeds. Founded in 1958, the BPS has published a wide variety of books and booklets covering a great range of topics. Its publications include accurate annotated translations of the Buddha's discourses, standard reference works, as well as original contemporary expositions of Buddhist thought and practice. These works present Buddhism as it truly is—a dynamic force which has influenced receptive minds for the past 2500 years and is still as relevant today as it was when it first arose. A full list of our publications will be sent upon request with an enclosure of U.S. $1.50 or its equivalent to cover air mail postage. Write to:

The Hony. Secretary
BUDDHIST PUBLICATION SOCIETY
P.O. Box 61
54, Sangharaja Mawatha
Kandy • Sri Lanka